Tchaikovsky

Elizabeth Clark

Illustrations by Tony Morris

The Bookwright Press
New York · 1988

Great Lives

Beethoven
Louis Braille
Captain Cook
Marie Curie
Francis Drake
Einstein
Queen Elizabeth I
Queen Elizabeth II
Anne Frank
Gandhi
Henry VIII
Joan of Arc
Helen Keller

John F. Kennedy
Martin Luther King, Jr.
John Lennon
Ferdinand Magellan
Karl Marx
Mary, Queen of Scots
Mozart
Napoleon
Florence Nightingale
Elvis Presley
William Shakespeare
Tchaikovsky
Mother Teresa

First published in the
United States in 1988 by
The Bookwright Press
387 Park Avenue South
New York, NY 10016

First published in 1988 by
Wayland (Publishers) Limited
61 Western Road, Hove
East Sussex BN3 1JD, England

© Copyright 1988 Wayland (Publishers) Ltd

Phototypeset by Kalligraphics Ltd, Redhill, Surrey
Printed in Italy by G. Canale C.S.p.A., Turin

Library of Congress Cataloging-in-Publication Data
Clark, Elizabeth.
   Tchaikovsky / by Elizabeth Clark: illustrated by Tony Moris
      p. cm. – – (Great lives)
   Bibliography: p.
   Includes index.
   Summary: Presents a biography of the nineteenth-century
Russian composer.
   ISBN 0–531–18245–2
   1. Tchaikovsky, Peter Ilich, 1840–1893 – – Juvenile
literature. 2. Composers – – Soviet Union – – Biography – –
 Juvenile literature.
[1. Tchaikovsky, Peter Ilich, 1840–1893. 2. Composers]
I. Moris, Tony. ill.   II. Title III. Series. IV. Series: Great lives
(New York, N.Y.)
ML3930.C4C54 1989
780′.92′4- -dc19
[B]
[92]   88-50
                                                            C
                                                         AC M

10703

Contents

The popular composer

The musical works of Peter Ilyich Tchaikovsky, the nineteenth-century Russian composer, are among the best-loved of all time. The composer enjoyed remarkable success within his own lifetime, although his compositions were often unkindly received by the critics when they were first performed. Since his death, Tchaikovsky's music has continued to delight and move listeners all over the world.

Tchaikovsky was a composer in the Romantic tradition. He composed beautiful, memorable melodies. In addition, he was able to write skillfully for the orchestra by combining instruments in new and exciting ways. The depth of feeling and expression he could produce in his work has ensured the lasting popularity of his music.

Tchaikovsky was trained to compose using the techniques established in the Western world, outside Russia. His own musical idol was the Austrian composer Mozart. But he was strongly

influenced by Russian ideas and traditions. This appears in his use of folksong from the Ukraine (a part of Russia), and dark, brooding themes that, for him, represented the idea of fate.

Although Tchaikovsky enjoyed tremendous professional success, he was frequently unhappy. He suffered from bouts of depression and drank heavily. However, he could be excellent company and had many devoted friends.

Many people probably hear at least one piece of Tchaikovsky's music during their lives. The haunting theme from the ballet *Swan Lake*, the passionate music of the *Romeo and Juliet Fantasy-Overture* and the clash of piano and orchestra in the *First Piano Concerto*, have all become famous outside the concert hall and theater. And the rest of his work, including symphonies, ballets and operas, are performed all over the world.

However, it was not until the age of twenty-three that Tchaikovsky embarked on his successful musical career.

Works like the rousing 1812 Overture *and hauntingly ballet music have ensured Tchaikovsky's lasting popularity.*

A sensitive child

Peter Tchaikovsky was born on May 7, 1840 in Votkinsk, Russia. His family was wealthy and he enjoyed all the comforts that his father's position as government inspector of mines could provide. He was the second of six children born to Ilya Tchaikovsky and his second wife, Alexandra. He was particularly fond of his sister Alexandra (Sasha) and his twin brothers Anatol and Modest, but he was most devoted to his mother and his young French governess, Fanny Durbach.

At the age of five, Peter received piano lessons from Maria Markovna Palchikova, a freed serf. A year later he could play better than his teacher. The family owned an orchestrion – a mechanical contraption somewhat like a music box – which played songs from Mozart's opera *Don Giovanni* and operas by other famous composers. Tchaikovsky soon learned to imitate them on the piano.

Fanny Durbach described how the sensitive boy was deeply affected by music. Once he called

Left *The Tchaikovsky family in 1848. Peter is standing on the left.*

out in the night that he could hear music although the house was silent. "I can't get rid of it, it won't leave me in peace," the troubled boy cried, but the sounds were in his mind.

In 1848 Peter and his brother Nicholas were sent to the Schmelling School in St. Petersburg (now Leningrad), and later on Peter attended the School of Jurisprudence (law). When he was fourteen, he was devastated by the news that his beloved mother had died of cholera. Soon afterward, Peter began to compose music. He claimed that this helped to sooth his mind.

A new piano teacher, Rudolf Kundiger, thought the young Tchaikovsky showed signs of musical talent. But he later told the boy's father that he saw no signs of genius in his son and advised against encouraging him to became a professional musician.

Left *The young boy delighted the family with his musical skills.*

The bored clerk

In 1859 Tchaikovsky entered the Ministry of Justice in St. Petersburg as a clerk. At that time he had no idea of becoming a professional musician. He worked conscientiously at first, but soon became the victim of extreme boredom. The story has been recorded of how a colleague, chatting with the young man, watched in fascinated dismay as Tchaikovsky absent-mindedly tore an official document into strips, rolled these strips into pellets and swallowed them.

Although Tchaikovsky found his work tedious, he threw himself vigorously into a hectic social life. He made the most of every opportunity to attend the theater, opera and concert hall, and would often sit at a musical performance with the score on his lap, following every note. In this way, and by talking to friends, he broadened his artistic education and was introduced to new ideas. He also became something of a dandy at this time, reveling in the life of a fashionable young man-about-town.

In 1861 Tchaikovsky welcomed a chance to travel. He was asked

A court ball in St. Petersburg, Russia's social and cultural center.

to accompany a friend of his father on a tour abroad, and to act as interpreter. Tchaikovsky had a natural gift for languages – as a quick-minded little boy, he had rapidly learned French and German from Fanny Durbach. His knowledge of languages proved invaluable when the two men visited Germany, Belgium and Paris. They also visited London. Tchaikovsky later developed a great liking for the novels of Charles Dickens and he learned a little English.

A nineteenth-century view of the Bolshoi Theater in Moscow.

Returning to St. Petersburg, Tchaikovsky did not neglect his musical studies. He began to take lessons in harmony with the teacher Nickolay Zaremba. He had by this time become a skillful pianist and now devoted most of his spare time to music.

Below *Eager to learn, Tchaikovsky would follow the musical score at concerts.*

From Ministry to Conservatory

In September 1862, the Russian composer and pianist, Anton Rubenstein, became director at the new Conservatory of Music in St. Petersburg. Tchaikovsky's teacher, Zaremba, transfered his classes there. The young man continued to study while working at the Ministry of Justice to support himself financially. His father had lost a considerable sum of money in rash business ventures and was unable to assist

Above *Nicholay Zaremba, Tchaikovsky's teacher.*

Below *Tchaikovsky played the flute in the orchestra.*

his son, although he was not now "entirely opposed" the idea of his becoming a musician.

In Russia, in those days, it was quite common for hopeful artists, writers and musicians to be employed in secure positions in the Civil Service while at the same time devoting themselves to their art. Tchaikovsky felt this was unfair both to the employer and to the art. In 1863 he left his job and enrolled at the Conservatory as a full-time student.

At the Conservatory he studied composition with the awesome Rubenstein himself, and gave private lessons to pay his way. He learned to play the organ and also the flute, which he played in the Conservatory orchestra.

His early compositions were often criticized and he suffered from severe attacks of nerves when called upon to conduct. A fellow student and loyal champion of his work, Herman Laroche, described how Tchaikovsky conducted his *Overture in F* with his right hand, while supporting his chin with his left as though to keep his head from toppling off his shoulders from fright.

St. Petersburg, where Tchaikovsky spent his happy student days.

Having had his work *The Storm Overture* heavily criticized by Rubenstein in 1864, Tchaikovsky now had to prepare his graduation piece, setting to music "Ode to Joy," a poem by the German poet Schiller. This was performed at a prize-giving ceremony on January 12, 1866. Rubenstein was furious when Tchaikovsky was absent from the oral examination, owing to his nervousness. Nevertheless Tchaikovsky duly graduated from the Conservatory, having been awarded the silver medal.

Professor Tchaikovsky

Anton Rubenstein's equally talented brother, Nicholas, had founded what was to become the Moscow Conservatory of Music in 1860, and six years later he invited Tchaikovsky to join his staff as Professor of Harmony. Delighted at the prospect of employment, but sad to leave St. Petersburg, he agreed. His many letters to his family reveal his early homesickness. He described the first nerve-racking lecture, during which he was "terribly ill at ease." Two weeks later he wrote that he was improving and "managing to adopt a professional air." He held the post until 1878, teaching and composing.

Below *Kamenka, near Kiev, where Sasha lived.*

Above *The stirring folk tunes of peasant dances provided many musical ideas.*

He began his *First Symphony* ("Daydreams") in March. In July, overwork brought about a nervous breakdown. In August, Anton Rubenstein and Zaremba refused to perform the symphony unless changes were made in it.

Although disappointed, Tchaikovsky now worked on the *Festival Overture* to celebrate the marriage of the Czarevich and the Danish Princess Dagmar. When he received the Czarevich's appreciative gift of gold and turquoise cufflinks, he quickly sold them for much-needed cash.

To Tchaikovsky's relief the altered *First Symphony* was performed reasonably successfully. He had used Ukrainian folk songs in this work and these featured strongly in his first opera, *The Voyevoda*, begun in 1867. He visited his sister Sasha, now married and living at Kamenka, near Kiev in the Ukraine. There, he was able to build up his knowledge of Ukrainian folk song.

Tchaikovsky was a handsome and shy man. Women found him charming. When the leading singer of a touring Italian opera company, Désirée Artôt, showed interest in the composer, he admitted he returned her affection and even wrote of an engagement. However, when he learned the following year that Désirée had married a Spanish singer, he was not at all heart-broken. The only blow was to his pride. He was now very much absorbed by his involvement with nationalism.

Tchaikovsky's meeting with Désirée led to a brief romance.

Nationalism

Nationalism was a powerful movement throughout Europe in the nineteenth century. It sprang from people's fierce loyalty to their homelands and desire for independence from ruling nations. Great value was placed on the culture, traditions and unity of the native people of a country. Nationalists believed they had a right to be free, whether from the rule of another country or from the tyranny of their own native rulers. In Russia, beginning in 1825, a series of attempted revolutions against the harsh Czarist regime had finally, in 1861, won freedom for millions of serfs.

In the arts, the writer Alexander Pushkin, and the "father of Russian music," Michael Glinka, had embraced the nationalist cause. In St. Petersburg, a circle of composers with nationalist sympathies had formed a group to produce music that was essentially Russian. Nicknamed "The Five," they were Mily Balakirev, Alexander Borodin, César Cui, Modest Mussorgsky and Nicholas Rimsky-Korsakov.

A contemporary painting of a peasant uprising in the 1860s.

Tchaikovsky met Balakirev in 1868, and later he met the whole group. He was interested in their ideas but annoyed by their blunt

criticism of his works. Balakirev conducted Tchaikovsky's symphonic work *Fate* in 1869, but his unfavorable judgement provoked Tchaikovsky into destroying the score. However, advised by Balakirev, he composed his first masterpiece, the *Romeo and Juliet Fantasy-Overture,* and also began an opera, *The Oprichnik.*

Below *Tchaikovsky with "The Five." (L to R) Balakirev, Tchaikovsky, Mussorgsky, Cui, Rimsky-Korsakov and Borodin.*

"The Five" believed, as did Tchaikovsky, that Russian folksongs celebrated the ideals of peasant freedom, and they used folk melodies extensively in their work. The years 1870–74 marked the period of "high nationalism" for Tchaikovsky, but his music differed from that of the St. Petersburg group because of his training in Western techniques of composition at the Conservatory. He did not join the group, but he learned a great deal, musically, from its members.

Criticism and praise

Between 1871–76 Tchaikovsky's music met with very mixed reactions. Pieces popular with the public were often coolly received by the critics; when the critics praised warmly, the public perversely showed little interest. Tchaikovsky was extremely sensitive to criticism, but was easily elated by praise. He suffered greatly during these years of uncertainty.

Although his opera *Undine* was rejected, he was successful with his *Second Symphony* ("Little Russian"), and with the *Tempest Overture*. Spurred on by this, he entered his opera *Vakula the Smith* in a competition in 1874, only to find he was a year early with the entry and would have to await the result.

He traveled a great deal during this period, and spent much time with Sasha in Kamenka.

In 1874, in a famous incident, Tchaikovsky showed his recently finished *First Piano Concerto* to Nicholas Rubenstein, to whom it was dedicated. Rubenstein belittled the work, saying it was unplayable, vulgar and that some passages were copied from the work of other composers. Very shaken, Tchaikovsky rededicated it to the pianist Hans von Bülow, who played the dramatic work to rapturous audiences in Boston, Massachusetts, in the following year. Later the concerto was warmly received in Russia and Rubenstein adopted it into his repertoire.

In 1876 Tchaikovsky was very depressed, although pleased to have been commissioned to write the ballet *Swan Lake*. He traveled to Vichy in France for his health and visited Bayreuth, in Germany, where he met the

Left *Hans von Bülow, the celebrated pianist, pictured here in the role of conductor.*

composer Franz Liszt. Returning to Russia he learned that his opera *Vakula the Smith* had won the competition. But the public did not like it, although they acclaimed his *Third Symphony*. His work *Francesca da Rimini* was a great success. At last, Tchaikovsky appeared to be succeeding in his chosen career.

Above *The Davidov family. Tchaikovsky became "favorite uncle" to Sasha's children.*

Below *A scene from Tchaikovsky's best-loved ballet, Swan Lake.*

A mysterious patroness

Lack of money was a constant problem for Tchaikovsky. In 1876, however, he began a correspondence with someone who was soon to become a mysterious patroness. He received a letter from a Madame Nadezhda von Meck, commissioning some violin sonatas. She was a wealthy

*In 1876 Tchaikovsky (**below**) began a long pen-friendship with Mme von Meck (**far right**)*

widow who deeply loved music. Letters between the two were exchanged frequently. When in 1877 Tchaikovsky wrote to her desperately asking for financial help, she not only gave him money but also made him a yearly allowance of 6,000 roubles. Madame von Meck wanted him to be free of money worries so that he could concentrate on composition. But she made one strange condition – that they should never meet. Tchaikovsky managed to avoid her when she attended his concerts, but he met her accidentally on two occasions when they were on vacation in the same area. They hurried past each other in flustered silence.

Their revealing pen-friendship lasted for fourteen years. In his letters to Nadezhda von Meck, Tchaikovsky confided his private feelings to her and described his methods of composing. He dedicated his *Fourth Symphony* to her as "my dearest friend" and visited her estate during her absence. He wrote his *Violin Concerto in D major* with the help of her house musician, Kotek, who was an ex-pupil at the Moscow Conservatory.

Madame von Meck even conspired with Tchaikovsky to marry her son Nickolay to Tchaikovsky's niece, Anna Davidov, in 1884. They felt that the union of their relatives would draw them closer together.

In this strange relationship, Tchaikovsky and Madame von Meck were able to believe that the other was the ideal friend. Because they avoided meeting, their illusions were never shattered.

Below *Nineteenth-century Moscow, where Tchaikovsky worked for many years.*

Marriage and separation

The year 1877 was a difficult one for Tchaikovsky. In March, the ballet *Swan Lake* failed with the public. The dancers' performances were poor and the original score had been altered.

In April, he received a letter from a young woman, Antonina Ivanovna Milyukova, claiming to be an ex-pupil and declaring her love for the composer. For a time he put off her invitations to visit, but eventually called upon her in June. His decision to call on her was influenced by work he was carrying out on the opera *Eugene Onegin*. In the opera, the heroine Tatyana writes a love letter to the older man Onegin and is rejected. Tchaikovsky, moved by his heroine's plight, was sympathetic toward Antonina and proposed marriage to her within a week of their meeting.

They married on July 18. From the beginning it was a disaster. Tchaikovsky was homosexual and was unable to have a full married relationship with his wife. He left her to stay with relatives, only to return to her and suffer a nervous breakown.

Antonina agreed to a separation and Tchaikovsky left Russia. He settled in Clarens, in Switzerland, with his brother Anatol. Madame von Meck sent Tchaikovsky money to relieve his financial worries, and later he went on to visit cities in Italy and Austria.

Tchaikovsky was deeply depressed and feared that he could no longer compose. He returned to the Conservatory but resigned his post as Professor of Harmony there in 1878. Antonina continued to make life difficult for him.

Tchaikovsky had to face the fact that homosexuality was not acceptable in the society of his time. This made him deeply unhappy throughout his life. He had hoped by his marriage, not only to gain "respectability" and silence malicious rumors about himself but also to enjoy a comfortable companionship and avoid loneliness. Unfortunately, this was not to be.

Tchaikovsky and Antonina, after their ill-fated wedding.

Growing success

During the next seven years Tchaikovsky spent his time mostly at country estates, relaxing and composing. The *Capriccio Italien* and *Serenade for Strings*, produced in 1880, confirmed that he had not lost his musical skill.

He needed to be reassured after the failure of his opera *Eugene Onegin* the previous year. It had failed mainly because of a poor performance by the students of the Moscow Conservatory.

In 1880 Nicholas Rubenstein commissioned the *1812 Overture* for the Moscow Exhibition. This "loud and noisy" piece commemorated the retreat from Moscow in 1812 by Napoleon's armies. In this famous overture Tchaikovsky called for realistic sound effects in the form of cannonfire, to be detonated from the conductor's platform. The piece was finally performed at the consecration of a cathedral in Moscow in 1882.

Tchaikovsky's talent was winning him recognition. In 1881 he declined the offer of the directorship of the Moscow Conservatory, a post left empty when his dear friend Nicholas Rubenstein died. In the following year, Czar Alexander III attended his new opera *Mazeppa*, and later awarded him the Order of St. Vladimir. Two years later he became head of the Moscow branch of the Russian Musical Society.

In 1885 Tchaikovsky decided to settle down in a rented house near Klin, just outside Moscow.

He renewed his friendship with Balakirev, and, advised by him, composed the highly successful *Manfred Symphony*.

Three years later, in 1888, Tchaikovsky felt confident enough to undertake his first international tour. He visited Leipzig, Hamburg, Berlin, Prague, Paris and London, and met with huge success as both a composer and a conductor.

Tchaikovsky conducts the famous 1812 Overture, *which celebrates the retreat of Napoleon's troops from Moscow.*

The concert platforms of Europe

By 1888, Tchaikovsky was being hailed as a successful composer within his own lifetime. The Czar bestowed a further honor upon him in the form of a pension.

The following year, Tchaikovsky, encouraged by the success of his first international concert tour, set out on a second tour, conducting at Cologne, Frankfurt, Dresden, Geneva and Hamburg. He also visited Paris and performed in London, where he was as much impressed by the thickness of the fog as he was by the high standard of the orchestra. Everywhere he went, people were delighted with his music.

Later in his career, Tchaikovsky became an honorary member of the French Academy and received an honorary Masters Degree in Music from Cambridge University.

During these years, his time was divided between conducting and composition. In 1890 he produced his opera *The Queen of Spades*, with its bizarre plot about gambling and the supernatural. Earlier in the year, the ballet *The Sleeping Beauty* had been coldly received, much to Tchaikovsky's surprise and disappointment.

Tchaikovsky received a final blow in 1890, when Nadezhda von Meck wrote to inform him that she was bankrupt and could no longer continue sending him an allowance. She hinted at bringing the correspondence to an end. Tchaikovsky's bewildered replies were not answered, and he had to accept that the pen-friendship, during which about 1,100 letters had been exchanged, was over. He was deeply hurt. The loss of the allowance no longer mattered. What wounded him was the loss of a very dear friend.

Left and right *Two scenes from the* Sleeping Beauty, *Tchaikovsky's favorite ballet.*

An American welcome

In 1891, Tchaikovsky prepared to visit the United States, where his music had always been popular. But the composer was suffering from deep depression. This was made worse in April, when he learned in Paris of the death of his sister Sasha. He almost abandoned the long trip.

However, on his arrival in the United States, his rapturous reception and the hospitality of the American people soon helped to cheer him. Tchaikovsky appeared in four concerts in New York to celebrate the opening of what is now Carnegie Hall. He also conducted in Baltimore and Philadelphia. He wrote in a letter that he was sure he was ten times more famous in America than in Europe.

In May, Tchaikovsky departed, delighted with the visit but homesick for Russia. He returned home and continued work on his new *Nutcracker* ballet. He was eager to include a musical instrument completely new to Russia – the celeste. His fear that other composers might use the celeste first led him to adopt smuggling tactics.

Tchaikovsky settled into his last home in Klin in 1892. But he was restless. He traveled in Europe with his nephew and companion, Vladimir (Bob) Davidov, Sasha's son.

Tchaikovsky's arrangement of the *Nutcracker Suite* from his ballet had been an instant success in March, but the ballet did not fare so well. Disappointed and exhausted by recent hard work, the composer was now looking much older than his fifty-two years.

Right *The people of New York gave Tchaikovsky a rapturous reception.*

Left *Tchaikovsky's house at Klin.*

Fate and Freedom

Fearing that his skills were fading, Tchaikovsky began to compose his great and most moving *Sixth Symphony* (the "Pathétique"). He called it the dearest of his musical offspring and the most sincere of his works. Its four movements were based on the themes "life," "death," "love" and "disappointment."

The symphony was received coolly by the St. Petersburg audience, who were unmoved by it at its first performance in October 1893. Tchaikovsky did not live to see audiences share his own love for the "Pathétique." He died in St. Petersburg on November 6, officially of cholera, then raging in the city. Reports claimed he had developed the disease after drinking a glass of unboiled water. Recent evidence suggests that he may have committed suicide by taking poison, to stop the spread of scandal connected with his

After a brief, agonizing illness Tchaikovsky died in 1893.

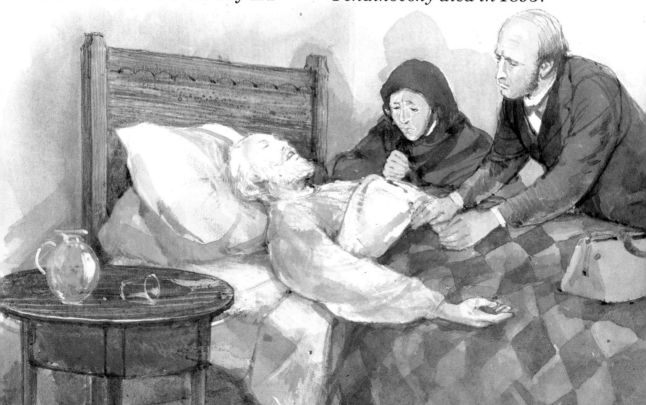

private life. On his death, he was sadly mourned and greatly honored by the Russian people.

Ideas of fate and freedom featured strongly in Tchaikovsky's life. He was obsessed with the idea of the individual's fight against fate, and this was the theme of many of his compositions. He believed equally passionately in the individual's right to be free,

The Tchaikovsky monument outside the Moscow Conservatory.

although he disapproved of revolution.

Struggling against what he felt was the harshness of his personal fate, Tchaikovsky believed that only through his music could he express himself truthfully.

Tchaikovsky described his sad life in this way: "To be sorry for the past, hope for the future and never be content with the present. That is my life." Nevertheless, he composed some of the most joyful music ever written. But it is the passion and the drama in his music that has moved generations of listeners and ensures that today he remains among the most popular composers of all time.

Important dates

1840   Peter Ilyich Tchaikovsky born in Votkinsk, Russia.
1848   Attends the Schmelling School in St. Petersburg.
1850   Enters School of Jurisprudence in St. Petersburg.
1854   Mother dies of cholera.
1859   Becomes first-class clerk at the Ministry of Justice.
1861   Tour of Europe.
       Studies harmony with Nickolay Zaremba.
1863   Enters Conservatory as full-time student.
1866   Takes up post as Professor of Harmony at Moscow Conservatory.
1868   Meets Balakirev and is later introduced to "The Five."
1869   *Romeo and Juliet Fantasy-Overture* written.
1870   The opera *The Oprichnik* begun. Opera *Undine* is rejected.
1873   *Second Symphony* and *Tempest Overture* performed with success.
1874   Opera *Vakula the Smith* entered for a competition a year early.
1875   *First Piano Concerto* played successfully in United States by Hans von Bülow.
1876   Visits Vichy for his health. Wins the competition in Russia with *Vakula the Smith*. Receives first letter from Madame von Meck.
1877   Disastrous marriage to Antonina Ivanovna Milyukova, leading to nervous breakdown. Madame von Meck becomes Tchaikovsky's patroness, making him an annuity. *Swan Lake* fails.
1878   Resigns from the Moscow Conservatory. Finishes the opera *Eugene Onegin*.
1880   Composes the *Capriccio Italien, Serenade for Strings* and works on *1812 Overture*.
1885   Rents a house at Klin. Becomes head of the Moscow branch of the Russian Music Society. Writes *Manfred Symphony*.
1888   First international concert tour of Europe. Receives a pension from the Czar.
1889   Second international concert tour.
1890   Production of *The Sleeping Beauty* and *The Queen of Spades*. Madame von Meck ends the correspondence with Tchaikovsky.
1891   Death of his sister Sasha. Successful visit to the U.S.
1892   The *Nutcracker* ballet is performed.
1893   Visits Cambridge University and is awarded an honorary Masters Degree in Music. October, *Sixth Symphony* ("Pathétique") performed. Dies on November 6.

Glossary

Concerto   A piece of music for one or more solo instruments and orchestra. It is usually in three contrasting movements (sections).

Critics   People who judge works of art. They are usually experts in their particular field.

Dandy   A man who is concerned with smartness of dress and appearance.

Harmony   The combination of musical notes.

Homosexual   A person (especially a man) who is sexually attracted to people of the same sex.

Nationalism   A movement based on patriotism and cultural identity, often producing a policy of national independence. It was particularly strong in nineteenth-century Europe.

Overture   A piece of music often played at the beginning of an opera or ballet.

Patroness   A woman who gives support, often financial, to a cause or to the arts, or to someone whose talent she wishes to encourage.

Repertoire   All the musical works that a musician has prepared and is competent to perform.

Romantic music   Most music composed between about 1830 and 1890, often inspired by a story, poem or painting, or by the composer's personal thoughts and feelings, following the Romantic movement in art and literature.

Score   The written or printed version of a piece of music.

Serfs   Slaves bound to the land, especially in Russia before 1861, the year in which they were emancipated (freed).

Sonata   A piece of music for solo instrument or a combination of instruments, usually in three or more movements.

Symphony   A musical work for orchestra, usually in four contrasting movements.

Theme   A group of notes forming a unifying melody, which is repeated and developed throughout a piece of music.

Ukraine   A large republic in south-east Russia, bordering the Black Sea. It has a long history and a rich cultural heritage.

Books to read

Lives of Great Composers by Ian Woodward. Merry Thoughts, 1969.

Swan Lake by Donna Diamond. Holiday House, Inc., 1980.

Tchaikovsky by Percy M. Young. David White, 1968.

Peter Tchaikowsky by Opal Wheeler. E. P. Dutton, 1953.

You can learn about Tchaikovsky's music from information on record covers. These tell a little about his life and give interesting information about particular compositions.

Index

Picture credits

Aquarius Picture Library 24; BBC Hulton Picture Library 7; Mary Evans 1, 8, 12
(upper), 16, 19; Novosti 9, 10, 11, 12 (lower), 14, 17, 18, 29.